Anonymous

Illustrated Guide to Fairmount Park and the Centennial

Exhibition Grounds and Buildings

Anonymous

Illustrated Guide to Fairmount Park and the Centennial Exhibition Grounds and Buildings

ISBN/EAN: 9783337193447

Printed in Europe, USA, Canada, Australia, Japan

Cover: Foto ©Lupo / pixelio.de

More available books at **www.hansebooks.com**

ILLUSTRATED GUIDE

TO

Fairmount Park

AND THE

CENTENNIAL EXHIBITION

GROUNDS AND BUILDINGS.

J. B. LIPPINCOTT & CO., PHILADELPHIA.

FAIRMOUNT PARK.

FAIRMOUNT PARK, new though it is, has already attained a reputation second only to that of Central Park, New York, and only second to that because Fairmount is not yet old enough to be as widely known.

Fairmount needs no eulogist. It speaks for itself; and the stranger who, with this book for his guide, will spend a summer day—or, better still, a week—in leisurely and appreciative exploration of its hills and dales, its leafy woodlands and sunny slopes, its rippling streams and placid river, its dewy sunrise and dreamy sunset, and the glory of its moonlight vistas, will permit no tongue to sound its praises louder than his own.

We preface our description of it with a few dry facts and figures which it will be well to bear in mind.

Fairmount Park arose from the necessity for a supply of pure water, the deterioration of

MONUMENT ERECTED TO THE MEMORY OF FREDERICK GRAFF.

which threatened to become not only an evil but a grievous calamity. The mills and manufactories on the banks of the Schuylkill were multiplying rapidly, and there was great danger that in the course of a very few years the river-banks for miles above the city would be lined with factories and workshops, to the utter ruin of the stream on which the citizens depended for their supply of pure water.

Just in time to prevent this catastrophe, Fairmount Park was conceived, and by degrees executed, until now five miles of the river and six of its beautiful and important tributary the Wissahickon, together with the high lands bounding their immediate valleys, are inclosed and preserved forever from all pollution and profanation.

The Park now contains nearly three thousand acres, being more than three times as large as the New York Central Park. It is dedicated to be a public pleasure-ground forever, and, under the management of a Board of Commissioners, is rapidly growing in beauty and interest.

EAST TERRACE, LEMON HILL.

The visitor will take a street-car on Pine, Arch, or Vine Street,—all of which lines run to the bridge at the lower end of the Park, while the two last named connect and run on to George's Hill, at its western extremity; or a car of the Green and Coates Streets line, which runs

THE LINCOLN MONUMENT.

from Fourth Street, *via* Walnut, Eighth, and Fairmount Avenue, to the Fairmount Avenue entrance; or a yellow car of the Union line, passing up Ninth Street and landing him at the

VIEW ON THE SCHUYLKILL, SHOWING THE BOAT-HOUSES AND LEMON HILL.

Brown Street entrance; or a Ridge Avenue car, which will carry him to the East Park; or, if well up town, a Poplar Street or Girard Avenue car, which will deposit him at Brown Street and Girard Avenue respectively. The Lancaster Avenue branch of the Chestnut and Walnut

CALLOWHILL STREET BRIDGE, AT THE FAIRMOUNT WATER-WORKS.

Streets line runs to the Centennial grounds in the West Park, and a branch of the Market Street line has been extended to the same point. All these termini, except the extreme western and northern ones, are in the immediate vicinity of Fairmount Water-Works, at the lower end of the Park. Another route is by the Park accommodation trains of the Philadelphia and Reading Railroad, which in summer run every hour during the day and carry passengers from the depot at Thirteenth and Callowhill to Belmont, on the west side of the Schuylkill. Accommodation trains on the Pennsylvania Railroad also run to Hestonville, within a short walk of George's Hill, at the western end of the Park.

Lastly, the visitor can hire a carriage by the day and make the tour of the Park without fatigue or difficulty; and for mere sight-seeing this is much the best way.

Entering the Park at the lower entrance, we step at once into the grounds pertaining to the Schuylkill Water-Works; and the works themselves are contained in the building, or rather group of buildings, just before us. These works were first put in operation in 1822, though the city was first supplied with water from the Schuylkill in 1799. Enormous engines worked by water-power force water from a dam in the river to the top of a hill in front of the building,—the original "Faire-Mount,"—where it is held in a distributing reservoir. The same works supply a reservoir on Corinthian Avenue, near Girard College. From a piazza in the rear of the building a good view is obtained of the new and elegant "double deck" iron truss bridge which has just taken the place of the once celebrated Wire Bridge. This new bridge is one of the most elaborate structures of its kind in this country. It was designed by J. H. Linville, and erected by the Keystone Bridge Company. The total length of the superstructure is 1274 feet, the main span, over the river, being 350 feet. The bridge has an upper and lower roadway and sidewalks, and is 48 feet in width; the upper roadway is elevated 32 feet above Callowhill Street, and connects Spring Garden Street on the east with Bridge Street on the west. The lower roadway connects Callowhill Street with Haverford Street.

FOUNTAIN NEAR BROWN STREET ENTRANCE.

The grounds immediately surrounding the buildings of the Water-Works contain several fountains and pieces of statuary. The monument in our cut is that of Frederick Graff, the designer and first engineer of the works. Just above the Water-Works is a little dock, whence in summer a couple of miniature steamers ply incessantly on the river, stopping at all points of interest on their route.

The main drive of the Park begins at Green Street, passing, just inside of the entrance, a new building designed for an art gallery, and thence running down nearly to the bank of the Schuylkill.

Next, crossing an open space ornamented by a bronze statue of Lincoln, erected by the Lincoln Monument Association, in the fall of 1871, we come to another hill, covered with trees, among which go winding paths, and under which green grass and flowering shrubs combine their attractions, while around the base of the hill flowers bloom and fountains play, and the

CONNECTING RAILROAD BRIDGE, FAIRMOUNT PARK.

curving drive leads a glittering host of carriages.   This is Lemon Hill, and on its summit is
the mansion in which Robert Morris had his home during the Revolutionary struggle.   Here
the great financier loved to dwell.   Here he entertained many men whose names were made

FAIRMOUNT PARK, FROM PENNSYLVANIA RAILROAD BRIDGE.

illustrious by those stirring times.   Hancock, Franklin, the elder Adams, members of the

ENTRANCE AT EGGLESFIELD.

Continental Congress, officers of the army and navy, and many of the foremost citizens met frequently under this hospitable roof. Here, busy in peace as in war, he afterwards planned those magnificent enterprises which were his financial ruin; and from here he was led away to prison, the victim of laws equally barbarous and absurd, which, because a man could not pay what he owed, locked him up lest he might earn the means to discharge his debt.

The fortunes of the once magnificent mansion have fallen, like those of its magnificent owner. It is now a restaurant, where indifferent refreshments are dealt out at correspondingly high prices; for it is an axiom that men pay most for the worst fare.

Next, following the carriage-drive, which, beginning at the Green Street entrance, runs up the river, we come to a third hill, formerly called "Sedgely Park." Here stands a small frame building known as "Grant's Cottage," because it was used by that general as his head-quarters at City Point. It was brought here at the close of the war.

From this hill there is an excellent view of the Schuylkill Water-Works, which stand in a ravine just beyond it. At its foot is the Girard Avenue Bridge, an elegant iron structure, the work of Clarke, Reeves & Co., of the Phœnix Iron Works, which connects the East and West Parks. This bridge was opened for travel July 4, 1874. It is 1000 feet long by 100 feet wide, and 52 feet above mean water mark. It consists of five spans constructed of Pratt trusses. The roadway is of granite blocks, and is 67½ feet wide, and the sidewalks, each 16½ feet wide, are paved with slate, with encaustic tile borders. The balustrade and cornice are ornamented

VIEW OF SWEET BRIER FROM EGGLESFIELD.

GIRARD AVENUE BRIDGE, FAIRMOUNT PARK.

with bronze panels representing birds and foliage. Under this bridge passes a carriage-way leading to the northeast portion of the Park, now called, by way of distinction, the East Park. The Connecting Railroad Bridge, as it is popularly termed, which unites the Pennsylvania Railroad with the Camden and Amboy, raises its graceful arches a little above the Girard Avenue Bridge, and through the rocky bluff which forms its eastern abutment a short tunnel has been cut, as the only means of opening a carriage-road to the East Park. This route was opened in the summer of 1871, and developed some of the loveliest scenery in all the Park. A number of fine old country-seats were absorbed in this portion of the grounds, and they remain very nearly as their former owners left them. Here a distributing reservoir, to cover one hundred and five acres, is now

VIEW ABOVE SWEET BRIER.

SCHUYLKILL BLUFFS, BELOW EDGELY.

being constructed. Continuing up this side of the river, we come finally to Laurel Hill Cemetery, and then to the massive stone bridge over which the coal-trains of the Reading Railroad pass on their way to Richmond.

We shall, however, find more marks of improvement by crossing the Girard Avenue Bridge into the West Park.

Below the Bridge, on the west side, is a tract called "Solitude," and in it stands an ancient house built by John Penn, son of Thomas Penn and grandson of William, and owned by his descendants until its purchase by the Park Commissioners. Just beyond this, the tall stand-pipe of the West Philadelphia Water-Works forms a conspicuous feature.

This tract, containing thirty-three acres, has been leased by the Park Commissioners to the Zoological Society of Philadelphia, which has

THE ELEPHANT HOUSE.

been managed so successfully that, although but a few years old, its collection is the finest in this country. No expense has been spared to perfect the Garden in every particular, and it is

CARNIVORA BUILDING.

THE MONKEY HOUSE.

f.tted up in a manner best suited for the maintenance and exhibition of birds and animals.
The Society intends establishing here a Zoological Garden second to none in the world, and is

THE BEAR PITS.

THE AVIARY.

rapidly carrying out its designs. It has agents in every part of the globe, from whom it receives frequent shipments of rare and interesting specimens of natural history, and is fast filling its

THE COLUMBIA BRIDGE, FROM THE WEST PARK.

grounds with specimens of every class of the animal kingdom. Every part of the garden is

SWEET BRIER RAVINE.

THE LANSDOWNE PINES.

interesting, but we may mention as the principal features the large and well-filled Carnivora and Monkey-Houses, the Bear Pits, the Aviary, and the Deer Park. All of these are already

LOOKING EAST FROM BELMONT.

well stocked, and are constantly receiving fresh accessions. The Garden was first opened to the public in July, 1874, and has already become one of the most popular features of the Park. The price of admission is 25 cents for adults, and 10 cents for children.

A short distance above the bridge is the Children's Play-ground, near Sweet Brier Mansion, and passing this the road enters Lansdowne and crosses the river road by a rustic bridge, from which the beautiful view of the Schuylkill shown in our engraving is had.

The venerable pines shown in our sketch mark the site of Lansdowne Concourse. This fine estate of Lansdowne contained two hundred acres, and was established by John Penn, "the American," whose nephew, also named John, the son of Richard Penn, built a stately mansion here, and lived in it during the Revolutionary war, a struggle in which his sympathies were by no means with the party that was finally successful in wresting from him the noble State which was his paternal inheritance and of which he had been Governor.

UP THE SCHUYLKILL, FROM COLUMBIA BRIDGE.

Leaving the Concourse, the road skirts the base of Belmont Reservoir, and, winding round a rather steep ascent, comes out on the summit of George's Hill, two hundred and ten feet above high tide.

This tract, containing eighty-three acres, was presented to the city by Jesse and Rebecca George, whose ancestors had held it for many generations. As a memorial of their generosity, this spot was named George's Hill, and its rare advantages of scenery and location will keep their name fresh forever. It is the grand objective point of pleasure-parties. Few carriages make the tour of the Park without taking George's Hill in their way, and stopping for a few moments on its summit to rest their horses and let the inmates feast their eyes on the view which lies before them,—a view bounded only by League Island and the Delaware.

In the broad meadow which lies at the visitor's feet as he stands on George's Hill, looking eastward, is the ground of the Centennial Exhibition, which is fully described a few pages farther on. We may here mention that George's Hill is a splendid site from which to overlook these grounds.

The carriage-road next brings us to Belmont Mansion. This, like most of the buildings in the Park, is of very ancient date, having probably been erected about 1745.

A VIEW ON THE WISSAHICKON.

This was the home of Richard Peters—poet, punster, patriot, and jurist—during the whole of his long life. Many of his witty sayings are still extant, as are also a number of his poems; while his eminent services as Secretary of the Board of War during the Revolution, Representative in Congress subsequently, and Judge of the United States District Court for nearly half his life, will not soon be forgotten. Brilliant as have been the assemblages of distinguished guests at the many hospitable country-seats now included within the bounds of Fairmount Park, the associations connected with Belmont Mansion outshine all the rest. Washington was a frequent visitor; so was Franklin; so were Rittenhouse the astronomer, Bartram the eminent botanist, Robert Morris, Jefferson, and Lafayette,—of whom a memento still remains in the shape of a white-walnut-tree planted by his hand in 1824. Talleyrand and Louis Philippe both visited this place; "Tom Moore's cottage" is just below, on the river-bank; and many other great names might be mentioned in connection with Belmont, if we had room for them. Now, alas! the historic mansion has degenerated into a restaurant.

FALLS BRIDGE, SCHUYLKILL RIVER.

The view from the piazza of the house is one which can scarcely be surpassed in America. Our engraving, though drawn by one of the first landscape painters in the country, gives but a faint idea of its beauty. It is one of those grand effects of nature and art combined which man must acknowledge his inability to represent adequately on paper.

Leaving Belmont, the road passes through a comparatively uninteresting section to Chamouni, with its lake and its concourse, and the northern limits of the Park. Near the lake it intersects the Falls road, and this takes us down to the Schuylkill, which we cross by a bridge, and continue up the east bank of the river to its junction with the Wissahickon.

One of the most beautiful walks in the Park extends from this point through Belmont Glen to the Reading Railroad and the banks of the Schuylkill. It debouches at the offices of the Park Commission, where the visitor's eye is attracted by a pair of colossal bronzes, representations of the winged horse "Pegasus."* These figures were made to adorn the Grand Academy in Vienna, but were found to be too large for the position assigned them. They were purchased by a number of American gentlemen, and presented to the Park; where they will eventually mount guard at one of the main entrances.

The Falls of Schuylkill exist only in history now, but before the Fairmount dam was built they were a beautiful reality. The cascade, which was formed by a projecting ledge of rock, was slight, but in seasons of high water it made a fine display.

A little above the Falls is the "Battle-Ground,"—the scene of an *intended* battle between the Americans under Lafayette and the British under General Grant. The latter, however, unlike his distinguished modern namesake, allowed himself to be outgeneraled, and Lafayette succeeded in executing a masterly retreat,—that being the only thing he could do under the circumstances. Here, also, was fought the memorable and disastrous battle of Germantown.

The Wissahickon is a lovely stream winding through a narrow valley between steep and lofty hills which are wooded to their summits, and have the appearance of a mountain-gorge hundreds of miles from civilization, rather than a pleasure-retreat within the limits of a great city.

In its lower reaches the stream is calm and peaceful, and boats are kept at the two or three small hostelries which stand on its banks, for the convenience of

WISSAHICKON CREEK.

those who wish to row on the placid waters. This calm beauty changes as the valley ascends, and we soon find the stream a mountain torrent, well in keeping with its picturesque situation and surroundings. So with alternate rush of torrent and placid beauty of calm reaches the romantic stream flows down from the high table-lands of Chestnut Hill to its embouchure in the valley of the Schuylkill.

A few manufacturing establishments have invaded the sequestered valley; but the Park Commissioners have taken measures to do away with them all after a certain number of years,

* Since transferred to the entrance to Memorial Hall.

2

UP THE WISSAHICKON—MEGARGEE'S PAPER MILL.

and restore the Wissahickon as nearly as possible to its pristine wildness and unfettered beauty. One of these invaders—Edward Megargee's paper mill—is shown in our illustration. Like most of the others, it is now owned by the city, but will be operated by the heirs of its late owner until the year 1882, after which it will be removed.

THE WISSAHICKON—BRIDGE AT VALLEY GREEN.   THE WISSAHICKON—BRIDGE NEAR MT. AIRY

THE PIPE BRIDGE OVER THE WISSAHICKON.

We may briefly notice a few of the many points of interest in this romantic glen, some of which our artists have sketched in a manner which renders pen-and-ink descriptions superfluous.

Soon after leaving the Schuylkill, the drive up the Wissahickon passes the "Maple Spring" restaurant, where a curious collection of laurel-roots deftly shaped into all manner of strange or familiar objects, the work of the proprietor, will repay a visit.

A little above this, a lane descends through the woods to the Hermit's Well, which is said to

PRO BONO PUBLICO.

UP THE WISSAHICKON.

have been dug by John Kelpius, a German Pietist, who settled down here, with forty followers, two hundred years ago, and lived a hermit's life, waiting for the fulfillment of his dreams. He and his associates gave names to many of the scenes about here, among them the Hermit's Pool, of which we give an illustration.

Three and a half miles above its mouth the stream is crossed by a beautiful structure called the Pipe Bridge, six hundred and eighty-four feet long and one hundred feet above the creek. The water-pipes that supply Germantown with water form the chords of the bridge, the whole

THE WISSAHICKON AT CHESTNUT HILL.

being bound together with wrought-iron. It was designed by Frederick Graff, and constructed under his superintendence. A hundred yards above this is the wooden bridge shown in our engraving. Near this is the Devil's Pool, a basin in Creshein Creek, a small tributary of the Wissahickon.

The next point of interest is the stone bridge at Valley Green, and half a mile beyond this is the first public drinking-fountain erected in Philadelphia. It was placed here in 1854, and was the precursor of a numerous and beneficial following.

UP THE WISSAHICKON—THE DRIVE.

A mile and a half of rugged scenery ensues, terminating in the open sunlight and beautiful landscapes of Chestnut Hill, where the end of the Park is reached.

Watson, in his "Annals of Philadelphia," speaks thus of "The Wissahickon:"

"This romantic creek and scenery, now so much visited and familiar to many, was not long since an extremely wild, unvisited place, to illustrate which I give these facts, to wit: Enoch and Jacob Rittenhouse, residents there, told me in 1845 that when they were boys the place had many pheasants; that they snared a hundred of them

THE WISSAHICKON—THE HERMIT'S POOL.

HEMLOCK GLEN.

MOUNT PLEASANT.—FORMERLY OWNED BY BENEDICT ARNOLD.

GLEN FERN, WISSAHICKON.

in a season; they also got many partridges. The creek had many excellent fish, such as large sunfish and perch. The summer wild ducks came there regularly, and were shot often; also, some winter ducks. They then had no visitors from the city, and only occasionally from Germantown. There they lived quietly and retired; now all is public and bustling,—all is changed.

The natural beauties of Fairmount Park are now its chief attraction, but these can be greatly enhanced by the discreet addition of works of art in the shape of statues, fountains, busts, etc. We are happy to state that a society under the name of the Fairmount Park Art Association has recently been established with the object of facilitating this adornment, and already embraces a large number of prominent citizens among its members. It should be the pride of every citizen to encourage its efforts. This Association has already erected several handsome bronze pieces, and placed a fine marble statue and several paintings in the Art Gallery in the Park.

THE CENTENNIAL EXHIBITION GROUNDS AND BUILDINGS.

In the selection of Philadelphia as the place where the Centennial Exhibition should be held, two important and desirable results were reached: it placed the Exhibition at the "birthplace of liberty," and secured one of the most eligible sites for the purpose in the country. Rich in historical associations, easily accessible from all points, and embracing a plateau affording ample space for the main and incidental buildings, Fairmount Park presents every feature that could be desired.

The Centennial grounds cover 236 acres, and extend from the foot of George's Hill almost to the Schuylkill River, and north to Columbia Bridge and Belmont Mansion. They can be reached directly by the following lines of horse-cars: Chestnut and Walnut, Market, Arch, Race and Vine, and Girard Avenue; and by steam-cars via the Reading Railroad and the Pennsylvania Railroad.

Approaching the Exhibition grounds by way of Elm Avenue, we first enter the MAIN BUILDING, which is 1880 feet long, 464 feet wide, 48 feet to the cornice, and 70 feet to the roof-tree, covering an area of 20 acres. At each corner a square tower runs up to a level with the roof, and four more are clustered in the centre of the edifice, and rise to the height of 120 feet from a base of 48 feet square. These flank a central dome 120 feet square at base, and springing on iron trusses of delicate and graceful design to an apex 96 feet above the pavement,—the exact elevation of the interior of the old Capitol rotunda. The transept, the intersection of which with the nave forms this pavilion, is 416 feet long. On each side of it is another of the same length and 100 feet in width, with aisles of 48 feet each. Longitudinally, the divisions of the interior correspond with these transverse lines. A nave 120 feet wide and 1832 feet long—said to be unique for combined length and width—is accompanied by two side avenues 100 feet wide, and as many aisles 48 feet wide. An exterior aisle 24 feet wide, and as many high to a half-roof or clere-story, passes round the whole building except where interrupted by the main entrances in the centres of the sides and ends, and a number of minor ones between. The iron columns supporting the roof number, in all, 672.

A breadth of 30 feet is left to the main promenades along and athwart, of 15 feet to the principal ones on either side, and of 10 feet to all the others. The

MAIN BUILDING.

MACHINERY HALL.

berths of the nations run athwartship, or north and south as the great ark is anchored. The classes of objects are separated by lines running in the opposite direction. Small balconies of observation are the only galleries of the Main Building. Those at the different stages of the central towers are highly attractive to students who prefer the general to the particular, or who, exhausted for the time, retire to clear their brains from the dust of detail and muster their faculties for another charge on the vast army of art. From this perch one may survey mankind from China to Peru.

Four miles of water- and drainage-pipe underlie the 21½ acres of plank floor in this building. The pillars and trusses contain 3600 tons of iron. The contract for it was awarded in July, 1874, and it was completed in eighteen months, being ready for the reception of goods early in January last. The cost was $1,600,000.

Leaving the Main Building at its west end, we pass to MACHINERY HALL, little smaller than its neighbor, it being 1402 feet long by 360 feet wide, covering an area of 14 acres. The main cornice is 40 feet in height upon the outside; the interior height being 70 feet in the two main longitudinal avenues and 40 feet in the one central and two side aisles. The avenues are each 90 feet in width, and the aisles 60, with a space of 15 feet for free passage in the former and 10 in the latter. A transept 90 feet broad crosses the main building into that for hydraulics, bringing up against a tank 60 by 160 feet, whereinto the waterworks precipitate, Versailles fashion, a cataract 35 feet high by 40 wide.

The substitution of timber for iron demands a closer placing of the pillars. They are consequently but 16 feet apart "in the row," the spans being correspondingly more contracted. This has the compensating advantage, æsthetically speaking, of offering more surface for decorative effect, and the opportunity has been fairly availed of. The coloring of the roof, tie-rods, and piers expands over the turmoil below the cooling calm of blue and silver. The external appearance of Machinery Hall is fully as pleasing as that of the building we just left. The one central and four terminal towers, with their open, kiosk-like tops, are really graceful, and the slender spires which surmount them are preferable to the sheet-iron turrets. Owing to the necessity of projecting an annex for hydraulic engines from one side of the middle, the building is distinguished by the possession of a front. The cost of the construction of Machinery Hall was $800,000.

Machinery Hall has illustrated, from its earliest days, the process of development by gemmation. Southward, towards the sun, it has shot forth several lusty sprouts. The hydraulic avenue which we have mentioned covers an acre, being 208 by 210 feet. Cheek by jowl with water is its neighbor fire, safe behind bars in the boiler-house of the big engine; and next branches out, over another acre and more, or 48,000 square feet, the domain of shoes and leather under a roof of its own.

Including galleries, and the leather, fire, and water suburbs, this structure affords more than

AGRICULTURAL BUILDING.

15 acres of space. We can here become learned in the biography of everything a machine can create, from an iron-clad to a penknife or a pocket-handkerchief. In the centre of the immense hall stands the demiurgos of this nest of Titans, an engine of 1400 horse-power, and the largest hitherto known.

Following Belmont Avenue, the Appian Way of the Centennial, to the northwest, we

HORTICULTURAL HALL.

penetrate a mob of edifices, fountains, restaurants, government offices, etc., and reach the AGRICULTURAL BUILDING,—the palace of the farmer. The building is worthy of a Centennial agricultural fair: 540 by 820 feet, with 10½ acres under roof, it equals the halls of a dozen State cattle-shows. The style is Gothic, the three transepts looking like those of as many cathedrals. The nave is 125 feet wide, with an elevation of 75 feet. The materials of this

BRIDGE OVER LANDSDOWNE RAVINE.

bucolic temple are wood and glass. The contract price was $300,000. Its contents are more cosmopolitan than could have been anticipated when it was planned.

Besides the indoor portion of the world's farmsteading, a barnyard of corresponding magnitude is close at hand, where all domestic animals are accommodated, and the Weirs, Landseers, and Bonheurs can find many novelties for the port-

folio. A race-track, too, is an addendum of course.

From this exhibition of man's power over the fruits of the earth and the beasts of the field, we cross a ravine where the forest is allowed to disport itself in ignorance of his yoke, and ascend another eminence to HORTICULTURAL HALL.

No site could have been more happily chosen for this beautiful congress-hall of flowers. It occupies a bluff that overlooks the Schuylkill 100 feet below to the eastward, and is bounded by the deep channels of a pair of brooks equidistant on the north and south sides. Up the banks of these clamber the sturdy arboreal natives as though to shelter in warm embrace their delicate kindred from abroad. Broad walks and terraces prevent their too close approach and the consequent exclusion of sunlight.

For the expression of its purpose, with all the solidity and grace consistent with that, the Moresque structure before us is not excelled by any within the grounds. Entering from the side by a neat flight of

HORTICULTURAL HALL—INTERIOR VIEW.

steps in dark marble, we find ourselves in a gayly-tiled vestibule 30 feet square, between forcing-houses each 100 by 30 feet. Advancing, we enter the great conservatory, 230 by 80 feet, and 55 high, much the largest in this country, and but a trifle inferior in height to the palm-houses of Chatsworth and Kew. A gallery 20 feet from the floor carries us up among

MEMORIAL HALL.

the dates and cocoanuts. The decorations of this hall are in keeping with the external design. The dimensions of the building are 380 feet by 193 feet.

Outside promenades, four in number, and each 100 feet long, lead along the roofs of the forcing-houses, and contribute to the portfolio of lovely views that enriches the Park. Other prospects are offered by the upper floors of the east and west fronts; the aërial terrace embracing in all 17,000 square feet. Restaurants, reception-rooms, and offices occupy the two ends. The cost of the building was $250,000.

A few years hence this winter-garden will constitute a great attraction at the Park. It will by that time be effectively supplemented by 35 surrounding acres of out-door horticulture.

Leaving Horticultural Hall, we cross the bridge spanning the picturesque

JUDGES' PAVILION.

Landsdowne Ravine to MEMORIAL HALL, which, as its name implies, contemplates indefinite durability. What Virginia and Massachusetts granite, in alliance with Pennsylvania iron, on a basis of $1,500,000, can effect in that direction, seems to have been done. The façade is in ultra-Renaissance, with arch and balustrade and open arcade. The square central tower, or what under a circular dome would be the drum, is quite in harmony with the main front in proportion and outline, and renders the unity of the building very striking. That its object, of supplying the best light for pictures and statuary, is not lost sight of, is evidenced by the fact that three-fourths of the interior space is lighted from above, and the residue has an ample

WOMEN'S PAVILION.

supply from lofty windows. The figures of America, Art, Science, etc., stud the dome and parapet, while eagles with wings outspread decorate the four corners of the corner towers.

The eight arched windows of the corner towers, $12\frac{1}{2}$ by 34 feet, are utilized for art-display.

GOVERNMENT BUILDING.

Munich fills two with stained glass: England also claims a place in them. The iron doors of the front are inlaid with bronze panels bearing the insignia of the States.

That the art-section of the Exposition would fill a building 365 by 210 feet, affording 89,000 square feet of wall-surface for pictures, must, when first proposed, have struck the most imaginative of the projectors as a dream. The actual result proved it indispensably necessary to provide an additional building of very nearly equal dimensions, or 349 by 186 feet, to receive the contributions offered, and this after the promulgation of a strict requirement that "all works of art must be of a high order of merit."

This building is on the rear, or north side, of Memorial Hall proper, and is the first portion of the fine-art department that meets the eye of one coming from Horticultural Hall. It is built of brick instead of the solid granite that composes the pile in front of it. In interior plan the extension closely imitates the main building.

MINOR BUILDINGS.—We shall now turn from the strictly public buildings to the more

PENNSYLVANIA BUILDING.

numerous ones which surround them, and descend, so to speak, from the capitol to the capital.

Directly opposite the entrance, but beyond the north line of the great halls, stands the *Judges' Pavilion*. In this capacious "box," 152 by 115 feet, the grand and petit juries of the tribunal of industry and taste have abundant room for deliberation and discussion.

Place aux dames ! First among the independent structures we must note the *Women's Pavilion*. To the trait of modesty the building has added that of grace. The interior, however, is more light and airy in effect than the exterior. The ground-plan is very simple, blending the cross and the square. Nave and transept are identical in dimensions, each being 64 by 192 feet. The four angles formed by their intersection are nearly filled out by as many sheds 48 feet square. A cupola springs from the centre to a height of 90 feet. An area of 30,000 square feet strikes us as a modest allowance for the display of female industry.

Uncle Sam confronts the ladies from over the way, a ferocious battery of fifteen-inch Rodman guns and other monsters of the

NEW JERSEY BUILDING.

same family frowning defiance to their smiles and wiles. The *Government Building* was erected to "illustrate the functions and administrative faculties of the government in time of peace, and its resources as a war-power." To do this properly, he has found two acres of ground none too much. The building, business-like and capable-looking, was erected in a style and with a degree of economy creditable to the officers of the board selected from the Departments of War, Agriculture, the Treasury, Navy, Interior, and Post-Office, and from the Smithsonian Institution. Appended to it are smaller structures for the illustration of hospital

and laboratory work. In the rear of the lordly palace of the Federal government stand the humbler tene- ments of *the States*. A line of these, drawn up in close order, shoulder to shoulder, is ranged, hard by, against the tall fence that incloses the grounds. In this row are em- braced Ohio, Indiana, Illinois, Wis- consin, Michigan, New Hampshire, Connecticut, Massachusetts, and Delaware. New Jersey and Kansas stand proudly apart, officer-like, on the opposite side of the avenue ; the regimental canteen, in the shape of the Southern Restaurant, jostling them rather closely. Ohio's pavilion plays the leading grenadier well ; but little Delaware, not content with the obscure post of file-closer, swells

NEW YORK BUILDING.

at the opposite end of the line into dimensions of 90 by 75 feet, with a cupola that, if placed at Dover, would be visible from half her territory. Pennsylvania's picturesque building stands on the south side of Fountain Avenue. Her Educational Department is represented by another building, near Memorial Hall.

These buildings are all of wood, with the exception of that of Ohio, which exhibits some of

OHIO BUILDING.

the fine varieties of stone furnished by the quarries of that State. All have two floors, save the Massachu- setts cottage, a quaint affair modeled after the homes of the past. The State of New York plays orderly sergeant, and stands in front of Delaware. She is very fortunate in the site assigned her, at the junction of State Avenue with several prom- enades, and her building is not un- worthy so prominent a position.

From the Empire State we step into the domain of Old England. Three of her rural homesteads rise before us, red-tiled, many-gabled, lattice-windowed, and telling of a kindly winter with external chim- neys that care not for the hoarding of heat. It is a bit of the island

peopled by some of the islanders. *Great Britain's* headquarters are made particularly attract- ive, not more by the picturesqueness of the buildings than by the extent and completeness of her exhibit.

Japan is a close neighbor to England. Besides the dwelling for its employés, the Japanese government has erected in a more central situation, close to the Judges' Pavilion, another building. The style of this is equally characteristic. Together, the two structures do what houses may toward making us acquainted with the public and private ménage of Japan.

The delicacy of

BRITISH BUILDINGS.

the Asiatic touch is exemplified in the wood-carving upon the doorways and pediments of the

JAPANESE BUILDING.

Japanese dwelling. Arabesques and reproductions of subjects from Nature are executed with a clearness and precision such as we are accustomed to admire on the lacquered-ware cabinets and the bronzes of Japan.

In the neat little *Swedish* School-house, of unpainted wood, that stands next

to the main Japanese building, we have another meeting of antipodes. This school-house is

attractive for neatness and peculiarity of construction. It was erected by Swedish carpenters.

The contemporaries and ancient foes of the Northmen have a memorial in the beautiful Alhambra like edifice of the Spanish government. *Spain* has no architecture so distinctive as that of the Moors, and

FOUNTAIN OF THE CATHOLIC TOTAL ABSTINENCE UNION.

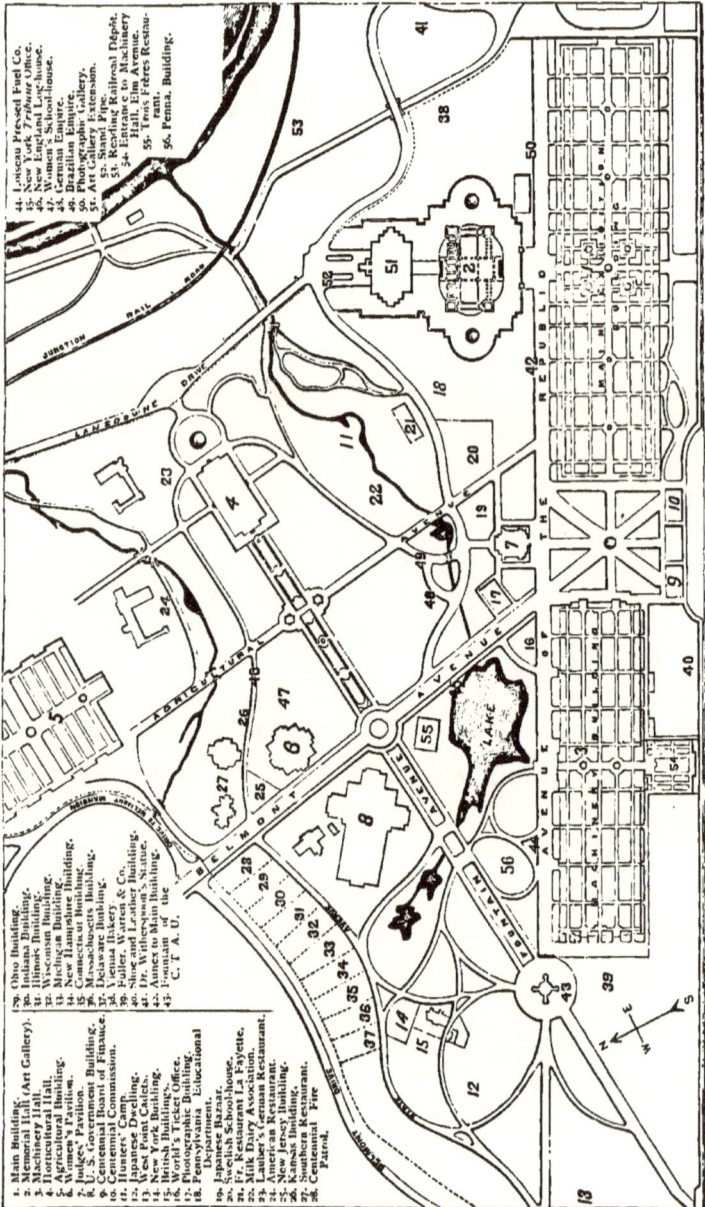

PLAN OF EXHIBITION GROUNDS.

1. Main Building.
2. Memorial Hall (Art Gallery).
3. Machinery Hall.
4. Horticultural Hall.
5. Agricultural Building.
6. Women's Pavilion.
7. Judges' Pavilion.
8. U. S. Government Building.
9. Centennial Board of Finance.
10. Centennial Commission.
11. Hunters' Camp.
12. Japanese Dwelling.
13. West Point Cadets.
14. New York Building.
15. British Buildings.
16. World's Ticket Office.
17. Photographic Building.
18. Pennsylvania Educational Department.
19. Japanese Bazaar.
20. Swedish School-house.
21. Fr. Restaurant La Fayette.
22. Dairy Association.
23. Lauber's German Restaurant.
24. American Restaurant.
25. New Jersey Building.
26. Kansas Building.
27. Southern Restaurant.
28. Centennial Fire Patrol.
29. Ohio Building.
30. Indiana Building.
31. Illinois Building.
32. Wisconsin Building.
33. Michigan Building.
34. New Hampshire Building.
35. Connecticut Building.
36. Massachusetts Building.
37. Delaware Building.
38. Vienna Bakery.
39. Fuller, Warren & Co.
40. Shoe and Leather Building.
41. Dr. Witherspoon's Statue.
42. Annex to Main Building.
43. Fountain of the C. T. A. U.
44. Loiseau Preseel Fuel Co.
45. New York *Tribune* Office.
46. New England Log-house.
47. Women's School-house.
48. German Empire.
49. Brazilian Empire.
50. Photographic Gallery.
51. Art Gallery Extension.
52. Stand Pipe.
53. Reading Railroad Depot.
54. Entrance to Machinery Hall, Elm Avenue.
55. Trois Frères Restaurant.
56. Penna. Building.

the selection of their style for the present purpose was in good taste. Seated not far from the Spainish building, and side by side with that of *Brazil*, are the handsome *German* buildings. The larger building is appropriated especially to the use of the German Commissioners; the two smaller ones are devoted chiefly to the exhibition of wines and chemicals.

France is represented by three small structures,—one for the general use of the French commission, another for the special display of bronzes, and the third for another art-manufacture for which France is becoming eminent,—stained glass. This overflowing from her great and closely-occupied area in Memorial Hall, hard by, indicates the wealth of France in art. She is largely represented, moreover, in another outlying province of the same domain,—photography.

Photographic Hall, an offshoot from Memorial Hall, and lying between it and the Main Building, is quite a solid structure, 258 feet by 107, with 19,000 feet of wall-space.

SWEDISH SCHOOL-HOUSE.

Among the most striking and unique buildings is the "*World's Ticket and Inquiry Office*," of Cook, Son & Jenkins, the world-renowned Tourist and Excursion Managers, shown in our illustration. The enterprise and connections of this firm are wonderful: no matter in what portion of the civilized earth, no matter what the language may be, "Cook's Tickets" are the sure guide for the stranger.

SPANISH BUILDING.

Their combination of tickets and excursions as displayed at their office, both for the United States and all parts of the world, show a very thorough system, the result of 35 years' practical experience.

It is not remarkable in this age that the most ambitious effort of monumental art upon the Exposition grounds should have taken the shape of a fountain. The erection is due to the energy and public spirit of the *Catholic Total Abstinence Union.* The site chosen is at the extreme western end of Machinery Hall. It looks along Fountain Avenue to the Horticultural Building. Mated thus with that fine building, it becomes a permanent feature of the Park. Other fountains are scattered through the grounds, but they are of comparatively modest proportions.

Another contribution in the cause of art is the statue, in bronze, of Dr. Witherspoon, the only clerical Signer, which stands on the east side of the grounds.

We have now briefly described the most important buildings which stand out prominently

3

in the midst of a host of structures of infinite variety of size, shape, and purpose, among which restaurants of various nationalities are especially noticeable.   But in a work necessarily

GERMAN BUILDING.

so condensed as this it is impossible to enumerate all of these structures, and, indeed, we doubt if any description would convey an adequate impression of the scene: suffice it to say that they notably exceed the corresponding array at any of the European Expositions.   The accom-

COOK'S WORLD'S TICKET AND INQUIRY OFFICE.

panying plan will give the reader an idea of the relative positions of many of the buildings, and serve as a guide in making the tour of the grounds.

BLOOMSDALE.

GREAT, and varied to an extent almost unexampled elsewhere, are the natural resources and industrial interests of Pennsylvania.

In mineral and other deposits none can compare with her; in the mechanism and skill which converts her ores from their crude condition into the ponderous, delicate, or minute forms useful to man, her sons are not excelled within or without the Union.

The ingenuity of Pennsylvania artisans is, in every branch of industry, almost world-wide; her locomotives traverse every road in Europe, and her iron ships, afloat and being built (a comparatively new outlet for her enterprise making the Delaware the rival of the Clyde), are destined to spread her fame wherever American commerce reaches. In view of such well-earned reputation, with such mechanical and artistic record, how fitting it is her *tillage*, on which commerce, manufactures, and industry of every kind repose, should be esteemed noteworthy. It is pleasant to know that her fertile soil, her intelligent husbandmen, her crops, and flocks, and herds may be referred to as justly entitled to high discriminating praise. It is true we have not within our borders broad prairies like unto those of the Far West, nor its unctuous soil which knows no depth, and ever yields without exhaustion of fertility. We glory in the natural wealth of our sister States—their prosperity is ours as well; but in our mines of coal, and iron, and other minerals, in our ceaseless flow of oil, nature has dealt kindly by us also. The gold of California, the cotton of the South, the sugar of Louisiana and Texas, the silks and other fibres of the world, the spices and coffees of the tropics, the highest mechanism of Europe, its best efforts in the useful and fine arts, are all at our command; we have only to stretch forth our hands and grasp what has been so bountifully placed within our reach; what has been denied us in nature's profuse scattering we have gained by thoughtful, well-directed efforts in the rotation of crops, in the application of appropriate fertilizers, and other means intelligently directed to a desired end, until "Pennsylvania Agriculture" has become simply another term for high-farming and successful tillage, whilst those who, resident at distant points, seek the best, where it be the fine strains of animals which graze its rich pastures, or the seeds of grasses, cereals, or vegetables, bend their steps hitherward, and never go empty away.

On the Delaware, a few miles above Philadelphia, and adjoining that fertile tract known as Penn's Manor, a wise and discriminating reservation of the proprietary Governor, is BLOOMS-DALE, which we have selected as illustrative of the rural industry of Pennsylvania. This estate, we do not hesitate to say, has contributed, in an especially large degree, to the public good, by its products and by its eminent example also. Bloomsdale may be assumed a model of intelligent industry, systematic culture, and rural progress. It embraces within its bound-

aries, independent of outlying lands, five hundred acres devoted to the culture and product of *seeds*, known in every hamlet, almost on every farm-hold and country homestead, as "Landreth's,"—known almost equally well on the banks of the Missouri, the Mississippi, and the Ganges,—for it should be stated, to the business credit and reputation of the firm, that for three generations Landreth's Seeds have been annually shipped to India, and are preferred by Englishmen resident in Hindostan to the seeds of their own native land, our climate ripening them better than the humid air of England.

It is the modest motto of the proprietors of Bloomsdale that "Landreth's Seeds speak their own praise." They certainly cannot have done so with feeble voice, for not only are those broad acres taxed to their utmost productive power, but nearly approaching one thousand other acres in addition, owned, occupied, and cultivated by the firm, are devoted to seed-culture ; by this it is not intended to designate lands simply tributary, tilled by their owners who raise crops on contract, without direct control of those who have bargained for the product (as it is the custom with seed-merchants thus to obtain supplies), but immediate, active, personal care and supervision. Thus an idea may be conceived, though necessarily imperfect, of the activity of mind and energy called forth by such extended operations ; but system and order are ever triumphant, and in the case in point the adage is aptly illustrated.   With increased acreage has come increased reputation, and Pennsylvania may claim the credit, not a slight one we opine, of having conducted within her borders a seed trade larger than exists elsewhere (if lands be taken as the measure), not alone within the Union, but without as well. Europe, travelers assert, can exhibit nothing of like extent.   This is no idle boast, made in the interest of private enterprise or pride of commonwealth.

Independent of the numerous workmen employed on the estate,—many of whom have been life-long *attachés* of the establishment, occupying cottages on the premises, and as much at home as the proprietors themselves—a pleasing feature which it were well to imitate,—there are three steam-engines for thrashing, winnowing, and cleaning seeds, grinding feed, etc. ; a "caloric" for pumping ; and an admirably well-adjusted steaming apparatus for preparing food for the working-stock. But it may be still more worthy of note that, for a term protracted through several years, energetic experiments in *ploughing* by *steam* have been conducted by the Messrs. Landreth at Bloomsdale, using the direct traction-engine of Williamson, with Thomson's India-rubber tire. At first, and for months, great hope of success was entertained ; but unforeseen difficulties in the way of direct traction exhibited themselves. At present the purpose is to adopt the "Rope System," as successfully practiced in England, using the Williamson engine as the motive power. It is simply right to chronicle their efforts in this direction. As the early efforts in river and ocean navigation are referred to with ever-increasing interest as progress is made in that direction, so will in the future be those of *tillage by steam*, and our State is entitled to its due share of praise with respect to land, as it unquestionably is to Fitch's exertions in steam navigation.

Limited space prohibits many of the details of the operations at Bloomsdale, which we would gladly give our readers ; the sketch annexed may, however, convey some idea of the extent of the structures required for the storage, drying, and preservation of crops, and otherwise successful prosecution of the peculiar business there conducted, which is a credit to the proprietors, the successors of those who founded the business in 1784, and which may be classed as prominent among the many industrial enterprises of Pennsylvania.

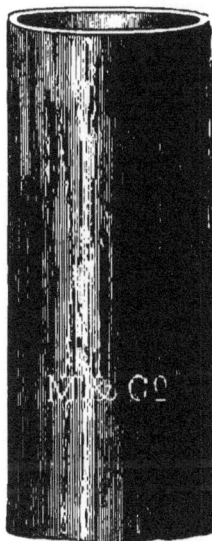
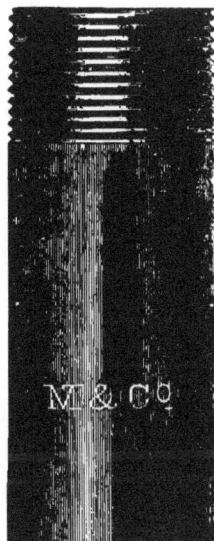

THE OLD PENN MUTUAL.

There is in the public mind an under-strata of clear, good sense, touching vital questions in general. While gaudy demonstrations of any kind will always attract a considerable amount of patronage and applause, the fact still remains that the public, as a whole, appreciate that the most which has in it the greatest substantial good. And life insurance is no exception to this rule. Those companies which have the most of evident integrity and enduring worth are those which in the long run secure constantly increasing favor at the hands of the people. To the operation of this rule is manifestly attributable the growing success which attaches to any of the companies which are now before the public, and most overwhelmingly is it true in the case of the Penn Mutual Life Insurance Company.

This Company justly ranks as one of the most reputable in all essential points in the country. It is ripe in years, grandly conservative yet justly liberal in management, and so evidently straightforward and conscientious in its course of action as to be singularly free from the criticisms and taunts which so often appear against insurance companies.

Our attention has been especially drawn to it upon this occasion through the appearance of its *twenty-eighth* annual statement, recently published. The Company increased in assets largely, in the amount of receipts over that of 1874, in the insurance in force, in the number of policies issued over the number of the previous year, and most decidedly in the matter of its net condition. In other words, notwithstanding the dull times of 1875, and the general falling off of the life insurance business, the Penn is not only to-day much richer in net condition, but much richer also in gross condition, than at any previous period of its history. To those familiar with the business it is not necessary to suggest the significance of an exhibit which shows, upon the New York basis of reserve, a surplus over liabilities of nearly twenty per cent. of the gross assets. Yet this is what the Penn Mutual shows, its assets being on January 1st, $5,504,329.24, and its liabilities on a four and a half per cent. reserve, $4,421,238.00, leaving a surplus of $1,083,091.24. On a four per cent. basis the liabilities are $4,756,438.00 and the surplus $747,891.24,—nearly fifteen per cent. of the gross assets. This showing is of course equally remarkable with the other, and reflects the highest honor upon the Company. The assets were increased during 1873, $913,565.69, and its surplus (New York standard) some $350,000. Its total income was about $400,000 larger than during the previous year, and its total expenditures were only $158,529 greater. On the other hand, the dividends paid to policy-holders during 1875 were several thousands of dollars greater than in 1874.   35m.

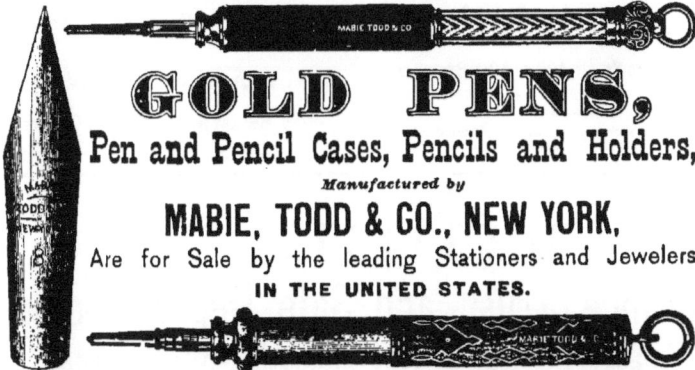

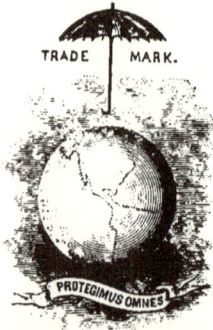

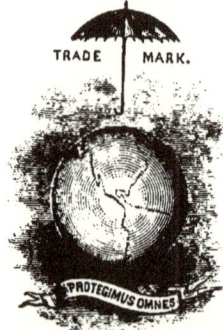

ZOOLOGICAL GARDEN,
FAIRMOUNT PARK, PHILADELPHIA.

This beautiful Garden, laid out with the greatest taste of the Landscape Gardener's Art, replete with Botanical and Floral beauties, and containing the largest collection of Beasts, Birds, and Reptiles in America, is **OPEN EVERY DAY.** Admission, 25 cents for adults, 10 cents for children. Accessible by all City Passenger Railways, and Schuylkill River Steamboats.

A Magnificent Restaurant is erected in the Garden,

where all the delicacies of the season, and substantial meals and refreshments, are served by Ferd. Hardt, who will make special contracts with excursionists, or serve by the card at moderate rates.

35m.

OF

GAS

IXTURES

SALESROOMS

1332 CHESTNUT STRE

OPPOSITE THE U.S. MINT.

MANUFACTORY 821 CHERRY

PHILADELPHIA.

W.D.S. Del

1332 CORNELIUS & SONS 1332

www.ingramcontent.com/pod-product-compliance
Lightning Source LLC
Chambersburg PA
CBHW030721110426
42739CB00030B/1047